DON'T PANIC

HOW TO CALM YOUR ANXIETY AND STAY CHILLED WHEN LIFE GETS STRESSFUL

Jasmin Kirkbride

INTRODUCTION

Nearly everyone will feel anxious at some point in their lives, but for some of us, it can be overwhelming, even rising up into nasty peaks called panic attacks. When anxiety takes hold, it can really feel like you're losing control.

But the truth is that you can master your thoughts. Even though anxiety can feel very real, your worries aren't true and, by turning towards your fears, you can begin to understand just how untrue they really are.

Facing your fears is an act of bravery, but you don't have to do it alone. This book is filled with simple tips and techniques to help you manage your panic and work through your worries. Though your anxiety might never completely go away, you can learn to manage it and live a more peaceful life. Best of all, you might just discover a really awesome person along the way: yourself.

MY ANXIETY MAKES ME VULNERABLE: MY RECOVERY MAKES ME STRONG.

WHAT IS ANXIETY?

Anxiety is a perfectly normal human feeling, just like anger, happiness or sadness. It's distinct from fear, because fear exists to warn us of a genuine danger in the moment, while anxiety focuses on something that is not objectively or immediately dangerous. You feel afraid if there is a speeding car coming towards you, for example, but you feel anxious about an exam or about going to an interview.

Fear and anxiety can feel quite similar, however, because they both put the body into a natural response called 'fight or flight' mode, where we're on high alert and packed with adrenaline. Because anxiety is a natural biological response, it is unlikely ever to go away entirely, but there are lots of things you can do to manage and accept it. These things allow you to rule your anxieties, rather than letting them rule you!

ANXIETY IS JUST
A PART OF ME.
IT IS NEVER THE
WHOLE STORY.

CAUSES OF ANXIETY

The things we feel anxious about can vary hugely and they don't always make sense – even when they're your own worries! It's normal to have a little bit of anxiety, but too much anxiety and it can feel like our emotions are spiralling out of control. When that happens, it's time to take action and tame the panic – which is exactly what this book is here to help with.

It can be comforting to remember that anxiety is the body's natural survival mechanism coming into play. It's just been tricked by our overactive brains into interpreting dangerous situations where they do not exist. Don't be hard on your body, your brain or yourself. Anxiety is natural and normal, but you don't have to let it run your life.

ANXIETY IS FEAR
OF ONE'S SELF.

WILHELM STEKEL

I DO NOT HAVE TO FEAR WHAT'S INSIDE.

HOW CAN STRESS CONTRIBUTE TO ANXIETY?

Stress has been called 'the epidemic of the twenty-first century', so if you're feeling snowed under, you're not alone. But just because everybody's feeling it, doesn't mean being super stressed out is OK. Stress occurs around particular events which put you under pressure, like tight deadlines or too much to do in one day. In reaction to the event, the body releases all sorts of chemicals to help us perform at our peak for an extended period of time. The side effects of these chemicals can include feeling anxious, and that anxiety can stick around after the thing that made us stressed has gone, especially if we are in the habit of feeling stressed. So, for many people, part of managing anxiety is also about managing stress.

I never have so much to do that I cannot take a break.

HOW CAN ANXIETY MANIFEST IN YOUR LIFE?

Like the things we worry about, there is no set rule for how anxiety 'should' be manifesting in your life. Every person experiences anxiety a little differently. In general, however, you might experience feeling sick in your stomach, muscle tension, heightened blood pressure, a fast or irregular heartbeat, pins and needles, light headedness or difficulty sleeping. Anxiety can also affect your thoughts: you might feel on edge, have a sense of dread, worry about other people knowing you are anxious, feel like your head is full of thoughts, have negative cycles of thoughts, feel restless, dwell on negative experiences or feel numb and disjointed from the world. You might also experience panic attacks, also known as anxiety attacks.

WHEN THE WALLS
CLOSE IN, I CAN
CHOOSE TO GIVE
MYSELF MORE
ROOM WITHIN.

If you're going through hell, keep going.

Winston Churchill

WHAT IS A PANIC ATTACK?

A panic attack is a sudden onset of intense fear or discomfort that will usually last for between five and twenty minutes. It normally includes a racing heart, sweating, trembling, pins and needles, light headedness or hyperventilation. You might also want to shout or cry quite a bit.

Many people who have had panic attacks say they felt completely out of control. Panic attacks can be an utterly overwhelming experience and your poor, worried mind can be convinced you're going to faint, cannot breathe, are having a heart attack, or are even going to die. The important thing to remember is that none of this is going to happen. Physically, panic attacks are not dangerous for your body, and they will pass. You are not going to die and you will regain control – you just have to ride out the storm.

Panic attacks are not a destination; they're just a bump in the road.

ANXIETY ON A SLIDING SCALE

Not only do people experience anxiety in different ways about different things, they also experience it to different degrees. Some people experience acute anxiety but only occasionally, while others experience a low level of worry almost all the time. Some people have a lot of anxiety, but have never actually had a full-blown panic attack. There is no rule of thumb: your experience of anxiety is just as valid as everyone else's. Whatever your anxiety levels, the tips in this book can help.

WHATEVER MY
EXPERIENCE IS
IN THIS MOMENT,
IT IS VALID.

ANXIETY AND MENTAL HEALTH

Some mental health conditions are associated with anxiety and, while you may not have or need a diagnosis of any of them, knowing about them can help you see your own experiences of anxiety from new angles. Here are some common forms of anxiety that you can look into in more depth for yourself. People with Generalised Anxiety Disorder (GAD) feel high levels of anxiety for long stretches of time, often without a specific reason. Panic Disorder is where people have ongoing, regular panic attacks. Obsessive Compulsive Disorder (OCD) causes repetitive compulsive actions or unwelcome cyclical thoughts.

Some people's anxieties are triggered by phobias, an intense and irrational fear of a particular object or situation. Post-Traumatic Stress Disorder (PTSD) can give you anxiety, flashbacks and nightmares after a horrible experience. Anxiety can also form a part of depression. If any of these symptoms sound familiar, don't worry, help is available, and with a little work, it is always possible to transform your relationship with anxiety.

MY **DIAGNOSIS** IS NOT A LABEL: IT IS A RELIEF FROM THE **UNKNOWN.**

SEEKING HELP

When it comes to anxiety or panic attacks, don't be afraid to seek help. Talking to someone can feel daunting but – like ripping off a plaster – it can be a freeing experience, particularly if you're at the end of your tether. Family and friends love you and they will be happy to lend an ear if you ask them to. If you feel you need more than that, you can always seek professional help too. The best way to start is by booking an appointment with your doctor and discussing the possibility of counselling or therapy. Don't forget that in an emergency, there are also a number of helplines available, including the Samaritans, who run a free 24-hour telephone service on: 116 123.

WHEN MY
SUPPORT
NETWORK IS
STRONG, IT
MAKES ME
STRONGER TOO.

**Be strong enough
to stand alone, smart
enough to know when
you need help, and brave
enough to ask for it.**

Ziad K. Abdelnour

YOU ARE NOT ALONE

Having high anxiety and panic attacks can be an isolating experience, but it's important to remember that you are not alone. Experts say that about one in ten people will experience a panic attack at some point in their lives and that about 15 per cent of the population has some kind of anxiety disorder, and those numbers continue to rise. You are not alone.

It can be tempting to blame ourselves for feeling anxiety, as if it's a fault, but the truth is anxiety can arise for all kinds of reasons and we shouldn't feel guilty about it. Acknowledging anxiety as an objective difficulty is key to overcoming it: your experience is legitimate and you don't need to feel bad about that. Embrace your feelings and breathe into them: there is nothing wrong with what you are going through.

BY ALLOWING
MY FEELINGS
TO BE, I AM
GIVING MYSELF
SPACE TO
BREATHE.

IN THE MOMENT: HOW TO DEAL WITH HIGH ANXIETY AND PANIC ATTACKS AS THEY HAPPEN

This section is designed to be a quick-fix guide to support you through tough moments of panic and anxiety. Once you've had a bit of practice, however, or if you'd like to go deeper, the sections after it can be a great help as well. Whenever or wherever anxiety strikes, just remember that panic is not dangerous – it is not going to kill you – and your scariest thoughts are never true. You can get through this and you are going to be OK.

The secret of change is to focus all of your energy, not on fighting the old, but on building the new.

Dan Millman

EVEN THOUGH ANXIETY FEELS TERRIBLE, IT WILL PASS AND I WILL FEEL BETTER.

ALLOW THE FEELING

First of all, it's very hard to deal with a panic attack if you're walking around denying it's happening. It's a bit like trying to find your way out of a room while refusing to open your eyes. Even though it feels counter-intuitive, if you feel yourself having a panic attack, relax into it. Let go of the idea that you won't have a panic attack. It's OK if you do. Sit back and allow it to happen. Stop thinking of panic and anxiety as 'bad' or 'wrong' and let them just 'be'. Acknowledging the reality of what you're feeling is the first step to moving through it.

POSITIVE OR NEGATIVE, I AM OK WITH WHAT I'M FEELING.

ONE STEP AT A TIME

When a panic attack strikes or your anxiety is through the roof, it can be hard to keep a handle on reality. When lots of different sensations are causing a number of scary thoughts in your brain, the effect can be completely overwhelming. When this happens, break the situation down into smaller chunks. Deal with one sensation at a time and one feeling at a time, working through them as slowly and calmly as you can. Remember your panic or anxiety is not dangerous, and your scariest thoughts are never true. This is not going to change, no matter how long you need to take to work through them.

JUST BECAUSE
I HAVE A
THOUGHT
DOES NOT
MEAN I HAVE
TO **BELIEVE** IT.

DOING JUST A LITTLE
BIT DURING THE TIME
WE HAVE AVAILABLE
PUTS YOU THAT MUCH
FURTHER AHEAD
THAN IF YOU TOOK NO
ACTION AT ALL.

BYRON PULSIFER

USE LOGIC

When anxiety strikes, it is often because your brain has short-fused and is using false reasoning to tell you the situation you are in is more dangerous or scary than it objectively is. Start to get back onto solid ground by telling yourself simple facts: your name, your age, your address. Remind yourself that you are having a panic attack or that you are anxious and that it will pass. Say it out loud if you find that helps. By asserting simple, logical truths, you are activating the part of your brain that understands that you can get through this and which is able to look after your practical needs in the meantime.

EVEN WHEN
I'M DROWNING
IN ANXIETY,
I CAN REMEMBER
TO SWIM TO A
LOGICAL SHORE.

BE OBJECTIVE

Once you are allowing your feelings and your 'logic' brain has been activated, focus on stepping back from your panic or anxiety. Let the feeling continue as it wants, but picture yourself stepping outside of its bubble. Let it go on without you in its centre. Instead of letting the feeling consume you, undertake activities that allow you to become an objective observer. Rate your anxiety on a scale from one to ten, where one is absolute calm and ten is the worst panic attack you can imagine. You might even want to make a joke: 'five out of ten, poor showing on light headedness, minus three points.'

I HAVE THE COURAGE
TO BECOME BIGGER
THAN MY FEAR.

Never trust your fears; they don't know your strength.

Athena Singh

BREATHING TECHNIQUES

When you're in the midst of a panic or anxiety attack, breathing correctly is one of the best things you can do to calm down. *Don't* breathe into a paper bag. Instead, focus on breathing slowly and deeply into your belly. Actively relax your muscles, keeping your posture loose but straight, and consciously move your diaphragm as you breathe. Soften your belly. Count in slow beats and breathe in an even cycle: in for five beats, hold for one, out for five beats, and hold for one.

Once you have established a breathing rhythm, start to count your breaths or, if you find that stressful, trace your thumb up one side of your index finger for an in breath and down the other side for the out. Trace each finger until you've reached the end of your hand, then work back towards your thumb. Keep going until you're calm.

A STEADY BREATH CAN CALM A TORNADO OF THOUGHTS.

If you want
to conquer
the anxiety of
life, live in the
moment, live
in the breath.

Amit Ray

HAVE AN AFFIRMATION

Like repeating those basic truths for your logical brain, having an affirmation to repeat to yourself can help bring you out of your anxiety cycle. Start with something basic, such as: 'I am a strong, sane person and this feeling will pass.' If you have a particular trigger for your anxieties, you might want to base your affirmation around that. Gently repeat it to yourself in moments of panic or anxiety to give you something to hold on to during the storm.

I am strong.
I am sane.
I can get
through
anything.

HAVE A SNACK

When did you last eat? It may sound strange but high anxiety levels and panic attacks can be triggered or made worse by low blood sugar levels. If you're totally stressed out, you may have forgotten to eat enough, causing your body to secrete extra adrenaline to keep itself going and leading to anxiety. Now's the time to eat. Start with some quick, sugary energy to bring you back up, but stick with gentle, natural sugars like fruit. Follow up with a high protein snack to stop you crashing once the sugar wears off and bring your body back to an even, normal blood sugar level. Have a large glass of water alongside your food, but sip slowly, don't glug. An anxious tummy is a delicate tummy and it's best to avoid shocking it.

**When I look after my body,
I take care of my mind.**

SIT IT OUT

Unless you are actively in danger, try to sit out your panic attack in the place it began. Environmental triggers can be a factor in anxiety, and it can be very helpful to prove to yourself that nothing bad is going to happen to you and that your anxieties aren't objective. What's more, sitting a panic attack out in the place it began means that you are less likely to develop negative thought cycles around that place, and it will be less likely to become a trigger for future panic attacks. Instead of running, find a place to sit and ride through the storm, knowing that, as the Buddhists say, 'This, too, shall pass.'

RUNNING AWAY PUTS OFF TODAY FEARS THAT I WILL STILL HAVE TO FACE TOMORROW.

Everything you want is on the other side of fear.

Jack Canfield

PRACTISE A MINDFULNESS EXERCISE

In moments of high anxiety, mindfulness exercises are a great way to ground yourself. To anchor yourself, breathe slowly and deeply into your belly, plant your feet gently on the floor, and focus your attention on the soles. Explore the sensation of your feet against the ground, through your shoes or directly if you're barefoot. Imagine a flow of strength coming up through the earth into your body and relax your legs and torso into it. Every time you think you've found out everything you can about the ground through your feet, breathe in deeper and find another detail to notice.

BY ANCHORING MY BODY, I GIVE BALLAST TO MY THOUGHTS AND THEY WILL SOON FOLLOW ME TO SOLID GROUND.

DON'T LET YOUR ANXIETY WIN

You can want to curl up and watch TV reruns all day after a panic attack, but one of the best things you can do is actually have a normal day. Go easy on yourself, but try to go to work, meet with friends, and get on with doing whatever you were planning to do. Anxiety can feel terrible, but by being strong in the face of it, you can stop it preventing you from living the life you want.

I will not let anxiety win.

Anxiety's like a rocking chair. It gives you something to do, but it doesn't get you very far.

Jodi Picoult

PREPARING FOR ANXIETY

Even though anxiety and panic attacks can strike seemingly out of the blue, there are safety nets you can put in place when you are feeling good to make sure that when they do pay a visit, you have ways of calming yourself quickly and effectively. By being prepared, you'll be able to face anxiety with confidence, and knowing you can beat it is half the battle.

ONCE I ACCEPT ANXIETY, I CAN STOP BEING SURPRISED BY IT.

MAKE A CUE CARD

Write a list of your first action points on a small card for when anxiety strikes. Your action points will change over time and should be tailored specially to you and the tricks you find work for you, but a good place to start is: *Stop. Allow the feeling. Breathe. Repeat your affirmation three times. Break down your worry into manageable sections. Challenge your thoughts one at a time.* Carry this card in your wallet or bag and bust it out when panic strikes, so that you can remind yourself how to cope even when you don't feel you can.

Expose yourself to your deepest fear; after that, fear has no power, and the fear of freedom shrinks and vanishes. You are free.

Jim Morrison

STOP. ALLOW.
BREATHE.
AFFIRM.
EXAMINE.
MOVE ON.

HAVE SOMEONE YOU CAN CALL

Even the strongest of us need help sometimes and for bad panic attacks some people can find it very helpful to call a friend. Ask a couple of family members or close friends to be points of contact when you're in need. You can also carry around the number of a helpline in case your chosen safety callers are busy. Try not to indulge the anxiety during the phone call, though. Talk about normal, safe topics to avoid spiralling further into your worries and draw yourself out of your thought cycles. Set a time limit on the phone call: hanging up shouldn't send you back into feeling panicky and alone, instead the call should be a bridge to your own strength when you really need it.

THE MOMENT I FEEL LIKE IMPLODING IS THE MOMENT I NEED TO REACH OUT.

TAKE A SNACK AND BOTTLE OF WATER WITH YOU

If you know that you are prone to moments of anxiety or panic, make sure you always carry a piece of fruit, a protein snack and a bottle of water with you. It's one less thing you will have to think about finding when your mind gets rocky, and it guarantees you a quick fix when you need it. Jerky, nuts, trail mix and snack-sized tins of fish all make for delicious and nutritious high-protein snacks, while apples and bananas are good, high-sugar fruits.

CURING THE MIND IS AS MUCH ABOUT LISTENING TO MY BODY AS MY BRAIN.

We cannot teach people anything; we can only help them discover it within themselves.

Galileo Galilei

HAVE SOME CALMING APPS ON YOUR PHONE

Remember that twenty-first-century stress epidemic? The upside of it for anxious people is that the digital world is full of great mindfulness apps, good for busting stress, worry and panic. Some popular free apps include Headspace, Calm, and Smiling Mind, but try out a few until you find one that works for you. Make sure you download a few of the exercises so that they're accessible in offline mode and take your headphones with you when you leave the house, so you can build your own private mindfulness retreat wherever and whenever anxiety strikes.

I CAN STEP BACK FROM MY **ANXIETY** WHENEVER I **CHOOSE.**

KEEP A JOURNAL

It can feel a bit scary, putting your fear in writing, but plucking up your courage to keep a private anxiety journal can be a very rewarding experience. Keep it simple: list your fear, where it happened, at what time, and how you got through your worrisome moment. Did you call a friend or get through it on your own? Was there a particular thought you found comforting or that helped put everything in perspective? If the fear came up again, how would you 'debunk' it? Not only will this journal help you rationalise your anxieties and let them go, but after a while you'll have an amazing record of all the fears you've overcome – that's quite a serious badge of bravery!

EVERY FEAR
I OVERCOME
IS ANOTHER
PROOF OF
HOW BRAVE
I AM.

Fortune always favours the brave.

P. T. Barnum

REARRANGE YOUR THINKING

Though panic attacks can have physical catalysts, they nearly always originate in that busy brain of yours! By examining how you think and changing it, you stop becoming the victim to your panic. Rather than reinforcing its strength over you, you begin to exert power over it. These tips are helpful in the long term, but they can also be crucial to maintaining a calm mind when panic strikes. By practising rearranging your thinking now, you will find your mind is stronger and better prepared to deal with your thoughts when they get tough.

FEAR IS A REACTION. COURAGE IS A DECISION.

WINSTON CHURCHILL

THE PATH TO A **PEACEFUL MIND** IS EASIER TO FIND WHEN I GRAB A MAP.

FEAR OF FEAR

People who suffer from high anxiety or panic attacks often find themselves becoming afraid of feeling anxious. But being afraid of anxiety doesn't change anything. In fact, if you wind yourself up and *expect* to be anxious, then it's more likely to happen! Working with this secondary layer of anxiety can be a challenge, but it's worth it. Don't chide yourself when you experience anxiety about anxiety. Instead, any time you notice yourself worrying about feeling anxious or having a panic attack, remind yourself of past bravery. Know that you will have the strength to get through it if it does happen. It can be hard to fight something invisible that only exists in your head, but instead of trying to run away, turn and face it. Your fears are never as bad as you think they will be once you're brave enough to look at them.

IT'S *OKAY* TO BE SCARED. BEING SCARED MEANS YOU'RE ABOUT TO DO SOMETHING REALLY, REALLY BRAVE.

Mandy Hale

EVEN THOUGH I CAN'T ALWAYS SEE MY OWN COURAGE, I KNOW IT'S THERE.

LIVE SHAME-FREE

You don't have to shout from the rooftops about your anxiety, but try to be honest with yourself about it. Be open with friends and family about your state of mind and what you need. The people who love you will want to help and understand. Anxiety is nothing to be ashamed of. It is a natural reaction of the human body to stressful situations and fears. Most people will experience anxiety at some point in their lives, and increasing numbers of us feel it more and more acutely. Don't be ashamed of your anxiety or your panic attacks – it is not your fault. It just is. By taking away anxiety's power to make you feel shame, you stop being its victim. Give yourself permission to have anxiety. Don't let your anxiety define how you feel about yourself. It's just a small part of a bigger, more beautiful picture.

I HAVE ANXIETY – IT DOES NOT HAVE ME.

IDENTIFYING YOUR PRESSURE POINTS

Anxiety is often caused by certain triggers. People can be afraid of all sorts of things – from spiders to going on stage – so there is no 'wrong' answer to the question of what makes you anxious. Some people have obvious triggers, while others may have a little more difficulty defining theirs. To find out what triggers you might have, it can help to keep a private anxiety journal: how anxious did I feel today?

Was there a specific cause? If there wasn't, can I think of a possible trigger? Presently, you will see patterns start to emerge.

Once you know your triggers, it is important not to indulge in actively avoiding them, as this will only give credit to your worries. Instead, use your new knowledge to help begin to understand your anxiety and exist with it more consciously. A conscious approach is an effective approach.

THE FIRST STEP TO UNDERSTANDING MY FEARS IS IDENTIFYING THEM.

ACKNOWLEDGE AUTOMATIC THINKING

When your brain gets into a state of anxiety, it engages in 'automatic thinking'. Automatic (and often untrue) thoughts pop into our heads, usually without us noticing. They repeat in cycles, sometimes for years, until they seem believable. In fact, automatic thoughts often contain false logic, or 'cognitive errors', especially when it comes anxiety.

An anxious mind produces three main types of cognitive error: emotional reasoning, catastrophising, and overestimating risk. The first step to tackling cognitive errors is to acknowledge they are there. Gently ask yourself: even if this thought feels real to me, is it objectively true? Mostly, you'll find, anxious thoughts are not true thoughts.

EVERY TIME YOU ARE
TEMPTED TO REACT
IN THE SAME OLD
WAY, ASK IF YOU WANT
TO BE A PRISONER
OF THE PAST OR A
PIONEER OF THE
FUTURE.

DEEPAK CHOPRA

My anxiety's only fear is perspective. It's time to make my worries afraid.

INTERROGATE YOUR FEARS

Anxious brains can think some ridiculous things are true, despite evidence indicating otherwise. This tendency can be made worse by emotional reasoning, which is the belief that a terrible event is more likely to occur because you are panicking, and overestimating risk, where your panicked brain thinks the risk of your fears happening is much bigger than it really is.

When panic or anxiety strike, bust out your inner scientist and get to work with some cold, hard logic. Interrogate your most upsetting thoughts by having a conversation with yourself, asking questions that you are only allowed to answer with facts, not opinions.

For example, rather than worrying your racing pulse is a heart attack, ask whether there's another explanation: have you recently exerted yourself? Is a panic attack more likely? You might still feel wobbly, but questioning this way will help you understand what's true, and what's just anxiety.

WHEN I AM
AFRAID, I SHOULD
ASK NOT WHAT
I *BELIEVE*, BUT
WHAT I *KNOW*.

TURN 'WHAT IF' TO 'SO WHAT'

Catastrophising is another cognitive error anxious minds indulge in. Not only do they think the worst will happen, they can also turn a situation into a catastrophe, when actually it would only be a minor inconvenience. Catastrophising thoughts often begin, 'what if…?' A great way to counter them is to turn that into a 'so what…!'

For example, 'What if my car breaks down? That would be a catastrophe' becomes 'So what if my car breaks down?' Calmly list the practical steps you would take if your fear happened, in this case perhaps calling roadside rescue and finding out if a nearby friend could drive to sit with you. Bring a sense of humour to your answers – catastrophising is a classic target for sarcasm – 'Poor me, perhaps I could even order takeaway and catch up on my favourite podcasts while I wait for the tow truck!'

You don't have to control your thoughts; you just have to stop letting them control you.

Dan Millman

SO WHAT IF
I HAVE ANXIETY?
I WILL
OVERCOME IT.

REFRAME PANIC AS SUCCESS

When working to improve anxiety, you are often asked to do things that seem very counter-intuitive: engage your fear, don't avoid it. Allow your panic, don't resist it. Perhaps strangest of all, celebrate your anxiety, don't see it as failure! Stop seeing a panic experience as a weakness, humiliation or failure. Instead, see the process of getting through it as the huge success and act of bravery it is. You can even have a list of rewards you are allowed to have when you experience strong anxiety: a special day out, a new game or a piece of clothing. Panic is not a failure and interrupting the idea that it could be instantly undermines it.

I GET TO DEFINE SUCCESS. SUCCESS IS HERE AND NOW, WHATEVER MY FEELING IS.

GET UNDER
THE BONNET

At the same time as it's important not to let your anxiety consume you, it can be an interesting and helpful experience to explore why it's there. Like anger and sadness, anxiety and panic are often our body's way of telling us there's something we're avoiding looking at. If you can't see the wood for the trees yourself, it can be helpful talking to friends or family. Alongside tips like those in this book and Cognitive Behaviour Therapy (CBT), talking therapy can also be very helpful for this. Opening up the bonnet to your head can seem scary, but inside it's a safe space: it's all just you, and you are lovelier than you know.

IT IS NOT ENOUGH TO
WALK AROUND MY
ANXIETY. I HAVE TO
WALK THROUGH IT.

FEAR IS THE BRAIN'S
WAY OF SAYING THAT
THERE IS SOMETHING
IMPORTANT FOR YOU
TO OVERCOME.

RACHEL HUBER

EXERCISE YOUR MIND

Mindfulness exercises can be very helpful for keeping your mind cool, calm and ready to action all these mental tricks effectively. There are lots of different mindfulness exercises out there and many different routines you can explore. However, a good start is to take ten minutes out when you first wake up and before you go to bed, just to breathe. Sit or lie in a comfortable position with your eyes relaxed and half open. Open your chest and soften your belly as you breathe deep, in and out. Watch your thoughts without judgement. Don't get caught up in them, just let them pass, like clouds in the sky. Your aim isn't to stop thinking, but just to slow your thoughts down. Mindfulness exercises like this assist in creating a safe space inside that you can use to help you examine a panic attack when it is happening.

BY CHANGING
MY HABITS ONE
BY ONE, I CAN
RESHAPE MY
MIND INTO A
SAFE SPACE.

WHY DO YOU
STAY IN PRISON,
WHEN THE DOOR
IS SO WIDE OPEN?

JALALUDDIN RUMI

ENJOY THE PRESENT MOMENT

During your mindfulness practice, or as an additional exercise, take time to notice the moment at hand. Anxiety and panic can often be caused by getting caught up in worrisome past events or imagined future catastrophes that will never come to pass. Instead of occupying your mind with these ideas, let yourself enjoy the present. Start by concentrating on your contact with the ground, on your feet and thighs if you're sitting down, or your back and legs if you're lying down. Slowly become aware of each part of your body, working from bottom to top, acknowledging how each bit feels without judgement. Then expand your awareness out, into the sounds and feelings in the world around you. Here, now, there is just you and the moment. There is nothing to fear, and nothing to worry about.

WORRYING ABOUT A PROBLEM WILL ONLY MAKE IT SEEM BIGGER.

Smile, breathe, and go slowly.

Thích Nhất Hạnh

LIVING TO LESSEN ANXIETY

Alongside rearranging your thinking and preparing for anxiety when it strikes, there are also lots of things you can do in your day-to-day life to lessen the occurrence of anxiety. These tips are not designed to add to your to-do list, or be another stress to whip yourself with. Don't give yourself a hard time if you can't change everything at once, just gently shift your habits towards living with more positivity and less stress.

**How I live defines
how I think.**

A BALANCED DIET

Eating a balanced diet helps balance your moods as well as keeping you healthy. Nutritional deficiencies can cause anxiety, so make sure you eat between five and seven fruit and vegetables every day, with starch like grains, potatoes, rice and pasta. Get plenty of protein through pulses, eggs, fish or chicken, and stay away from over-processed, high-sugar foods. Make sure you eat regularly to maintain even blood sugars and snack healthily on chopped fruit and raw veggies with dips.

Though vitamin supplements are no replacement for meals, take a trip to your doctor to make sure you don't have any deficiencies. A top-up of omega-3 and -6, iron, B vitamins, L-theanine and vitamin D in particular have been found to benefit anxiety sufferers.

Finally, drink two litres of water a day – water is the best and purest thing you can put in your body. Think pure body; think pure mind.

**Nothing can
bring you peace
but yourself.**

Ralph Waldo Emerson

Facing my anxiety means looking after my whole self, body and mind!

CUT BACK ON STIMULANTS

When it comes to stimulants, you are what you eat. Caffeine and sugary drinks will rapidly raise your blood sugars, then send them crashing – cue anxiety! The same goes for sugary foods like chocolate, cakes, biscuits and sweets. You don't have to cut out these stimulants completely or overnight, but be aware of what you're putting into your body and try to cut back. You might feel strange for a few days as your body adjusts, but you'll soon notice a difference.

On the other hand, alcohol is a depressant and, while it may briefly make you feel more positive, in the long run it actively disrupts good mental health patterns in your brain. Smoking also contributes to anxiety: nicotine replaces your natural ability to cope and as soon as you finish your cigarette, you enter into stressful withdrawal symptoms. Drugs are their own rollercoaster: just say no!

MY MIND
DOESN'T
NEED MORE
STIMULATION,
IT NEEDS MORE
KINDNESS.

EXERCISE REGULARLY

Exercise isn't just good for your body, it's good for your mind too. Physical activity produces endorphins, which help reduce stress, lower anxiety, and improve sleep. You don't have to go crazy at the gym or suddenly become a body builder: studies have shown that something as simple as a ten-minute walk each day can boost your mood.

Give yourself a gentle exercise schedule, with three thirty-minute sessions a week. Though classes can be a good way to find a sense of community within your exercise, you don't have to spend lots on joining a gym: cycling, running and exercise videos on YouTube are all effective, free ways to work out. Some find mindful exercises like yoga and Pilates calm the mind, while others get relief from taking up kickboxing or weight lifting. Try out lots of different activities and find something that you enjoy – after all, exercise should be fun!

DON'T CHAIN YOUR WORRIES TO YOUR BODY. THE BURDEN SOON BECOMES HEAVY AND YOUR HEALTH WILL GIVE TOO MUCH OF ITSELF TO PICK UP THE EXTRA LOAD.

ASTRID ALAUDA

I AM ALWAYS IMPROVING, EVEN WHEN I TAKE ONE STEP FORWARD AND TWO STEPS BACK.

GET ENOUGH SLEEP

To help you sleep, have a bedtime routine. Don't drink caffeine or sugary drinks in the evening as they'll keep you awake. Instead, take a calming magnesium or calcium supplement and try bathing to relax your muscles. Tuck up in bed, washed and in your PJs, half an hour before you want to sleep, so that you have time to unwind. Turn off technology, as the light from LED screens keeps you awake: try reading a book or listening to a podcast instead.

After half an hour, or when you get drowsy, turn out the light and snuggle in. Don't try too hard to sleep: just trust your body to get there naturally. Consciously relax your muscles one at a time, close your eyes, and breathe deeply and slowly. Allow thoughts to pass without judgement, just imagine them becoming part of your breath and let them go.

IT'S OK TO TRUST MY BODY AND LET IT REST.

LESS SCREEN TIME

Digital technology affects your mental health as well as your sleep. We all have to do a certain amount of screen time for work, but more and more studies are finding a link between overuse of technology and anxiety. You can counter this simply by limiting your screen time. You might even want to go on a digital purge and ban screens from your downtime for a few days or weeks.

Social media also comes with problems. While it can be a great way to stay in touch, it can create anxiety-causing fear of missing out and peer pressure, and is addictive. Text responsibly and use social media mindfully. Give yourself a certain number of logins per day and give each login a time limit. To help, try deleting social media from your phone and downloading apps to hide your news feed, or limit the time you spend on certain websites.

Some of us think holding on makes us strong; but sometimes it is letting go.

Hermann Hesse

EACH TIME
I STEP OUT INTO
THE WORLD,
I CAN CHOOSE
TO CREATE
A POSITIVE
REALITY.

TAKE REGULAR BREAKS

Heavy workloads, long hours sitting at a desk and tight deadlines are a fact of life. But if you push yourself for too long without giving your brain a rest, you will tire it out, making yourself irritable, tired and anxious. The antidote is to take regular breaks. Step away from your work for 5–10 minutes every hour. Gaze into the middle distance to rest your eyes, breathe deeply and go for a walk if you can. Make sure you take your lunch breaks too, and not at your desk. Though sometimes you have to put extra hours in to meet a deadline, try to keep evenings and weekends sacred. By giving your brain a break, you'll actually find your productivity rising as well!

IT IS OK TO LET GO. ESPECIALLY WHEN I AM CARRYING SOMETHING HEAVY.

GET ORGANISED

The environment we live in can have a huge effect on how we feel. If your room is dirty and your desk is a mess, it's likely that you will feel chaotic as well. Have a spring clean, throw out old things you don't want or need any more and organise your belongings so that your life can run smoothly and easily.

Have a to-do list that you can reasonably tackle. Break tasks down into small parts and have a checkbox for each one. The sense of achievement as you blast through them will make you feel like completing more. Keep a neat, clear calendar as well, either digitally or on paper, so that you know what to expect each day and can prepare for it in advance. Anxiety has a hard time gaining traction when you can see the road ahead.

Each day is
not a challenge
to overcome,
but an
adventure
to enjoy.

**Every day
brings a choice:
to practise stress
or to practise peace.**

Joan Borysenko

ASK FOR HELP
WHEN YOU NEED IT

Asking for help is not a failure, in fact it's a huge success: it shows that you know your limits and can keep a situation under control before it gets to breaking point. This is as true for work as it is for your emotional life. Turning to friends, family or colleagues when you need help is a sign of strength. Best of all, once you make that initial request, you will have the confidence to ask again in future, starting a virtuous cycle. Having help when you need it will allow you to be better able to assist those you love when they need it too: when life's weight is spread across everyone's shoulders evenly, the load doesn't seem so heavy.

WHEN I FEEL
MYSELF FALLING,
I CAN TRUST
THE WORLD TO
CATCH ME.

LEARN TO SAY NO

Anxiety is irrational, so it's important not to actively avoid your triggers. However there are still situations where you might want or need to say no for other reasons and that is valid.

Acknowledge when you're anxious about something and don't let the worry stop you, but also trust yourself to know when you can't take something on, or when a situation is no longer right for you. By saying a gentle 'no' you create room for unforeseen positive possibilities to bloom, and the more positivity you invite in, the less worried you become.

Keeping a sane workload is important to managing stress and anxiety levels, but so is keeping a low-intensity emotional schedule. Dinners and parties can be tiring, especially for people who experience social anxieties. Book in only as much as you are comfortable with and you'll find yourself having more fun when you do go out.

'No' is freedom.

The universe has no fixed agenda. There is no right or wrong, only a series of possibilities.

Deepak Chopra

SELF-CARE AND RELAXATION

It can be tempting to give yourself a hard time about having anxiety, but one of the biggest keys to overcoming it is to learn to love yourself despite – and even because – of your worries! Part of self-care is taking time out for rest and relaxation, so this section covers some helpful tips on how to recoup when anxiety's been on your case. By taking care of your body and mind, you can learn to love yourself step-by-step and piece-by-piece. Self-care is not optional; it's essential.

WHEN I LOVE MYSELF, I AM FREE.

GIVE YOURSELF PERMISSION TO CARE FOR YOU

Self-care and kindness from others can be hard to accept for anxiety sufferers because their worries often make them believe they are undeserving. Yet, because anxiety comes from having thoughts about yourself that are harsh and not true, when you practise loving-kindness towards yourself, it's a big slap in the face to your worries! Give yourself permission to believe you should be treated well – by everyone, but especially by you.

If you're having trouble accepting care and kindliness, try the following exercise: during your mindfulness practice, picture a glowing, soft-white light growing in your stomach. Fill this light with positivity and love, letting it spread and grow all over your body, until in your mind's eye you are a beautiful, shining being. Then let the love spill out into the world around you: your light is beautiful, and you deserve to let it shine!

NO MATTER HOW ANXIOUS I AM, I WILL BE KIND AND LOVING TOWARDS MYSELF.

COMPASSION IS
NOT RELIGIOUS
BUSINESS, IT IS
HUMAN BUSINESS;
IT IS NOT LUXURY, IT
IS ESSENTIAL FOR
OUR OWN PEACE AND
MENTAL STABILITY.
IT IS ESSENTIAL FOR
HUMAN SURVIVAL.

DALAI LAMA

THINK KINDLY

When you catch a horrible thought about yourself popping into your head, like 'I can't', 'I'm a failure' or 'They won't like me', take a moment to question it. Would you say such harsh things to a friend? Would you even think them about someone else? Do you have an evidence base to believe that about yourself? If you wouldn't say it to someone else, don't say it to yourself. Let the thought be, know that it's not real, and think something kind about yourself instead, before moving on with your day. Practise thinking kindly by standing in front of a mirror every morning and saying five new, kind things about yourself out loud. By allowing kindness, your relationship with yourself will burst positivity!

I DESERVE
TO BE LOVED
JUST AS MUCH
AS EVERYBODY
ELSE.

SOMETIMES WHAT FEELS LIKE BREAKING DOWN IS REALLY JUST BREAKING FREE.

CRISTEN RODGERS

DAILY AFFIRMATIONS

The affirmations you practise during a panic attack can benefit you in your day-to-day life as well. Write a series of positive affirmations to counter all those little, troubling thoughts you have. Use your thought-challenging techniques to come up with true, factual responses that are relevant and specific to you. It could be as simple as 'I am loved', 'I am strong' or the faithful, 'This will pass'. Over time, the positivity will start to shine through into your everyday experience.

The greatest weapon against stress is our ability to choose one thought over another.

William James

IT'S NOT ABOUT CHANGING MYSELF, BUT THE WAY I THINK ABOUT MYSELF.

START A CONGRATULATIONS AND HAPPINESS DIARY

Journaling isn't just for figuring out what your worries are, it's for recording the things that make you happy too. Start to keep a diary of all the things you're proud of. Try to come up with at least three things a day which required bravery or strength, or which you just did really well at. Some days it could be winning an award, others it could be getting out of bed – big or small, celebrate every success and congratulate yourself. As an additional practice, record one thing that has made you happy every day. For both tasks, try to be specific and not to repeat – every day is unique and so are your achievements!

A LITTLE MORE POSITIVITY EACH DAY WILL BUILD THE HAPPINESS HABIT OF A LIFETIME.

Looking back isn't going to help you. Moving forward is the thing you have to do.

McKayla Maroney

KNOW YOUR REWARDS

Have a reward scheme for when you successfully get through a panic attack or achieve something that has been making you anxious. Write a list of things you know make you feel good, from having a bath to tending the garden. Stay away from rewards that reinforce negative habits, like cigarettes or glasses of wine. While it can be fun to splurge out on a big reward like a new pair of shoes or a games console, it's just as valuable to enjoy simple, cheaper pleasures. Buy flowers, cook yourself an elaborate meal, light some candles, read a book, go the movies, have a bath, or dance in your living room – you can even splurge on an indulgent evening just for you – whatever your reward, know that you are worth it.

ONE DAY I WILL FEEL ENOUGH SELF-LOVE THAT I'LL FORGET I EVER DOUBTED MYSELF.

COMPLEMENTARY THERAPIES

While not run of the mill, many people find that complementary therapies can work well in conjunction with more traditional mental health techniques to improve anxiety. Acupuncture, reflexology and massage can benefit tired minds and bodies. Other treatments, like herbal remedies and aromatherapy, you can take at home: try a relaxing chamomile tea before bed and sprinkling your pillow with lavender oil to help you sleep, for example.

One of the best natural remedies of all for stress, anxiety and worry is a good laugh. Laughter boosts the happy chemicals your brain releases, actively lowering the stress hormone cortisol. Crack a joke with a friend, watch a comedy show, or listen to a funny podcast – laugh as much, as loudly, and as often as you can.

THE ROAD THAT IS RIGHT FOR ME IS THE ONE I SHOULD BE TAKING.

I'VE FOUND THAT THERE IS ALWAYS SOME BEAUTY LEFT – IN NATURE, SUNSHINE, FREEDOM, IN YOURSELF; THESE CAN ALL HELP YOU.

ANNE FRANK

GO GREEN

Getting out into nature has been shown to have a hugely beneficial effect on your mental state. Take a walk in your local park, take a trip to the beach, or simply tend your garden – so long as you are outside in the fresh air and the elements, you will be oxygenating your body and breeding positivity in your mind. Take time to relax, slow down to a gentle stroll, breathe deeply and really take in the beauty of the day. Let nature's own positivity seep in.

NATURE IS THERE
FOR ME IN
EVERY MOMENT,
ALL I HAVE TO DO
IS STEP OUTSIDE
MY FRONT DOOR.

MEET WITH FRIENDS

Human beings are sociable creatures and being alone all the time is a sure-fire way to give your anxieties free rein. When you're feeling low, it can be hard to believe hanging out with other people can make you feel better, especially if you suffer from social anxieties. But that's when it is most important to hang out with friends. Hang out with people who make you feel good about yourself and who support you. Don't be afraid to talk about yourself and answer honestly when they ask how you are. If having to have a conversation seems too much, organise to play a board game or watch a movie instead. Being around other people is one of the best things you can do to draw you out of yourself.

Friends can help each other. A true friend is someone who lets you have total freedom to be yourself – and especially to feel.

Jim Morrison

Friends remember the light in me, even when I have forgotten about it myself.

LISTEN TO CALMING, UPBEAT MUSIC

Music is real food for the soul, and busting out your favourite tunes is a sure-fire way to improve your mood. If your mind is spinning, pick a playlist that is calming and upbeat. If you're having trouble selecting, there are lots of playlists online that have been specifically curated for people with anxiety, and the band Marconi Union even released 'Weightless', a song specifically designed to calm and relax troubled minds. While you're listening, don't be afraid to try your mindfulness exercises or have a dance. Mindfulness and music go well together, while dancing will help your body and mind connect, releasing tension and building those positive vibes.

EVEN WHEN I DON'T HAVE **CONTROL OVER MY MIND**, I DO HAVE CONTROL OVER WHAT I PUT INTO IT.

INVEST IN YOURSELF

Self-care doesn't stop at the front door, try to employ it in every area of your life. Book the work training you've been wanting, join that fancy gym, ask out your crush – invest your time, money and energy in the things that make you feel better and happier. With every step you take to invest in yourself, you're contradicting your anxieties. This takes strength and courage, but the benefits are so worth it, because every door you open brings in a plethora of new possibilities.

Don't move the way fear makes you move. Move the way love makes you move. Move the way joy makes you move.

Osho

I AM
WORTH
THE
EFFORT.

STEP BY STEP, I WILL BECOME BRAVER, AND PIECE BY PIECE MY MIND WILL BECOME A LIGHTER SPACE.

CONCLUSION

Be patient with yourself. You are only human and anxiety is a normal part of human existence, but with these tips you'll be better prepared to face your fears. You may not be able to change your thoughts and habits overnight, but a slow drip feed of positivity will lessen how often and how acutely you feel your panic and anxiety.

Don't whip yourself with expectations about how you should be thinking and feeling; just breathe into each experience and every moment. What anxious people most need is gentleness – from themselves. Allow yourself to have bad days without judgement. Give yourself permission to be happy without worrying about whether fear is around the corner. Keep on investing in self-love and practising observing your thoughts and you will soon find it's possible to live without your anxiety in charge.

IT'S NO USE GOING BACK TO YESTERDAY, BECAUSE I WAS A DIFFERENT PERSON THEN.

Lewis Carroll

BELIEVE IN YOURSELF

Jasmin Kirkbride

£8.99

Hardback

ISBN: 978-1-84953-949-4

Do you ever wish you had more confidence in your abilities? Do you sometimes have negative thoughts, comparing yourself to others? Have you ever been afraid to speak up because you don't think your opinion is valid?

You are not alone, and there is a way to tackle your low self-esteem. Packed with tips, suggestions and quotes, this book will help give you the strength to turn negatives into positives and become more confident every day.

STRESS LESS

Jasmin Kirkbride

£8.99

Hardback

ISBN: 978-1-84953-910-4

When people tell you to chill out or stop worrying, do you wish they would just shut up? Because if it was that easy, you'd do it, right?

You are not alone, and there is a way to tackle your stress. Packed withtips, suggestions and quotes, this book will help give you the strength to beat the what ifs and worries and live a little more every day.

If you're interested in finding out more about our books, find us on Facebook at **Summersdale Publishers** and follow us on Twitter at **@Summersdale**.

www.summersdale.com